PET PERSPECTIVES

First Facts®

A HORSE'S VIEW

OF THE WORLD

by FLORA BRETT

CAPSTONE PRESS
a capstone imprint

First Facts are published by Capstone Press,
1710 Roe Crest Drive, North Mankato, Minnesota 56003.
www.capstonepub.com

LIBRARY OF CONGRESS CATALOGING-IN-PUBLICATION DATA

Brett, Flora, author.
A horse's view of the world / by Flora Brett.
pages cm.—(First facts. Pet perspectives)
Summary: "From a horse's point of view, tells about horse senses, providing
insight into horse behavior and abilities"—Provided by publisher.
Audience: Ages 5-7.
Audience: K to grade 3.
Includes bibliographical references and index.
ISBN 978-1-4914-5044-4 (library binding)
ISBN 978-1-4914-5086-4 (eBook PDF)
1. Horses—Juvenile literature. I. Title.
SF277.B66 2016
636.1—dc23   2014044747

EDITORIAL CREDITS

Carrie Braulick Sheely, editor; Tracy Davies McCabe, designer;
Katy LaVigne, production specialist

PHOTO CREDITS

Capstone Studio: Karon Dubke, 7, 17; Shutterstock: ashkabe, 15, Eduard
Kyslynskyy, 13, Elya Vatel, 19, Hanna Alandi, 21, Lenkadan, cover, 1, Maros
Bauer, 9, olgaru79, 5, smeola, 11
Design Element: Shutterstock: stoyanh

Printed in China by Nordica
0415/CA21500544
042015   008845NORDF15

TABLE OF CONTENTS

LET'S HEAR IT FOR HORSES!

Clop! Clop! Clop! Our **hooves** have been around a long time! Horses lived at least 50 million years before the first humans. We became **domestic** 5,000 years ago. Today we continue to be side by side with people. We race, pull **carriages**, and compete in all kinds of events.

More than 200 horse **breeds** exist throughout the world.

4

hoof—the hard covering on an animal's foot

domestic—tame; no longer wild

carriage—a vehicle with wheels that is usually pulled by horses

breed—a certain kind of animal within an animal group

THE WORLD THROUGH MY EYES

Can you see in two directions at once? I can! Each of my eyes has its own wide view. I can see almost all around me without turning my head. But I do have a blind spot behind me, so don't approach me from behind. If I don't see you coming, I may get scared.

My large eyes let me see even the smallest movement. That's why all the motion on a windy day can make me nervous.

SENSITIVE SENSES

My body is super **sensitive**! I can feel a tiny fly on my back.

My hearing is also sharp. I can hear sounds from several miles away. I lift my head and prick up my ears when I hear a sound. Then I turn my head to see where the sound is coming from.

Each of my ears hears separately from the other.

sensitive—
able to feel
things easily

9

NOSTRILS THAT KNOW

My sense of smell is very strong. These big **nostrils** will notice if there is something in my food that usually isn't there. When I meet another horse for the first time, I breathe into its **muzzle**. We get to know each other by smelling each other's breath.

Arabians (right) have larger nostrils than most other horse breeds.

nostril—an opening in the nose used to breathe and smell

muzzle—an animal's nose, mouth, and jaws

HANGING WITH THE HERD

We're all about friends and family! We're **social** animals and prefer to live together in **herds**. We rarely fight within our herd. But we will bite or kick one another to show who's in charge. We also enjoy the friendship and company of people and other animals, such as dogs.

If I get scared by something, my **instinct** is to run away. My long, strong legs allow me to run quickly.

social—living and doing things together in groups or packs

herd—a large group of animals that lives or moves together

instinct—behavior that is natural rather than learned

TALK LIKE A HORSE

I use sound to **communicate**. If I blow or snort, I might be afraid. If I **neigh** loudly, I might be looking for a nearby horse.

I also move my ears, flare my nostrils, and use other body language to communicate. If my ears point forward, I'm interested in what you're saying. Ears pointed back mean I'm angry.

My tail talks too! If I'm swishing it from side to side, I might be bothered by something. I put it straight out or high to show happiness or playfulness.

communicate—to pass along thoughts, feelings, or information

neigh—to make a long, high-pitched sound

15

HEALTHY HOME, HEALTHY HORSE

I depend on you to care for me. I need a lot of exercise. I like to spend time outside in a **pasture** every day. But I do need a **stall** or other type of **shelter** to keep me comfortable in bad weather. Remember to clean my stall regularly. I need lots of drinking water. Mainly I can eat grass and hay. But I may also need grain, especially in winter.

My hooves grow constantly, so they need to be trimmed regularly. If they grow too long, I could develop foot and leg problems.

pasture—land where farm animals eat grass and exercise

stall—the small area of a barn where a horse sleeps

shelter—a safe, covered place

TIPS ON TRAINING

When you ride me, tell me what you want by using your hands, legs, body weight, and voice. It will take time for us to understand and trust each other.

Spending a lot of time together also helps us get to know each other. When you're not riding on my back, I can learn a lot just by being around you.

Reward me with a carrot or apple to let me know I'm doing what you want.

AMAZING BUT TRUE!

You probably wouldn't be able to sleep standing up, but we can! The bones and **ligaments** in our bodies lock together. This ability relaxes us enough to fall asleep while standing. Standing keeps us ready to run away from any danger.

Horses sometimes sleep lying down. But heavy weight on their bones for too long can hurt them.

ligament—a tough, stretchy band of tissue

GLOSSARY

breed (BREED)—a certain kind of animal within an animal group

carriage (KAYR-ij)—a vehicle with wheels that is usually pulled by horses

communicate (kuh-MYOO-nuh-kate)—to pass along thoughts, feelings, or information

domestic (duh-MES-tik)—tame; no longer wild

flare (FLAIR)—to spread outward

herd (HURD)—a large group of animals that lives or moves together

hoof (HOOF)—the hard covering on an animal's foot

instinct (IN-stingkt)—behavior that is natural rather than learned

ligament (LIG-uh-muhnt)—a tough, stretchy band of tissue

muzzle (MUHZ-uhl)—an animal's nose, mouth, and jaws

neigh (NAY)—to make a long, high-pitched sound

nostril (NOSS-truhl)—an opening in the nose used to breathe and smell

pasture (PASS-chur)—land where farm animals eat grass and exercise

sensitive (SENS-i-tiv)—able to feel things easily

shelter (SHEL-tur)—a safe, covered place

social (SOH-shuhl)—living in groups or packs

stall (STAWL)—the small area of a barn where a horse sleeps

READ MORE

Eschbach, Andrea, and Markus Eschbach. *How to Speak Horse: A Horse-Crazy Kid's Guide to Reading Body Language and "Talking Back."* North Pomfret, N.J.: Trafalgar Square Books, 2012.

Ganeri, Anita. *Winnie's Guide to Caring for Your Horse or Pony.* Pet's Guides. Chicago: Heinemann Library, 2013.

Marsh, Laura F. *Ponies.* National Geographic Kids. Washington, D.C.: National Geographic, 2011.

INTERNET SITES

FactHound offers a safe, fun way to find Internet sites related to this book. All of the sites on FactHound have been researched by our staff.

Here's all you do:

Visit *www.facthound.com*

Type in this code: 9781491450444

Check out projects, games and lots more at
www.capstonekids.com

Critical Thinking Using the Common Core

1. Horses don't "talk" the way people do. Explain three ways horses communicate with people and one another. (Key Ideas and Details)

2. Long ago people used horses to do work on farms and to travel from place to place. Now horses are used mostly for people's hobbies, and people use cars, airplanes, and other vehicles to travel. What do you think the advantages and disadvantages of this change have been? (Integration of Knowledge and Ideas)

3. Why is it important to speak calmly to horses and not surprise them? (Key Ideas and Details)

INDEX